The Shifting Book for Cello

Part One: Shifting to 4th and 5th Positions

by Cassia Harvey

CHP171

©2006 by C. Harvey Publications All Rights Reserved.

www.charveypublications.com - print books
www.learnstrings.com - PDF downloadable books
www.harveystringarrangements.com - chamber music

I = A String   III = G String
II = D String   IV = C String

First to fourth positions

Cassia Harvey

The Shifting Book for Cello, Part One

12

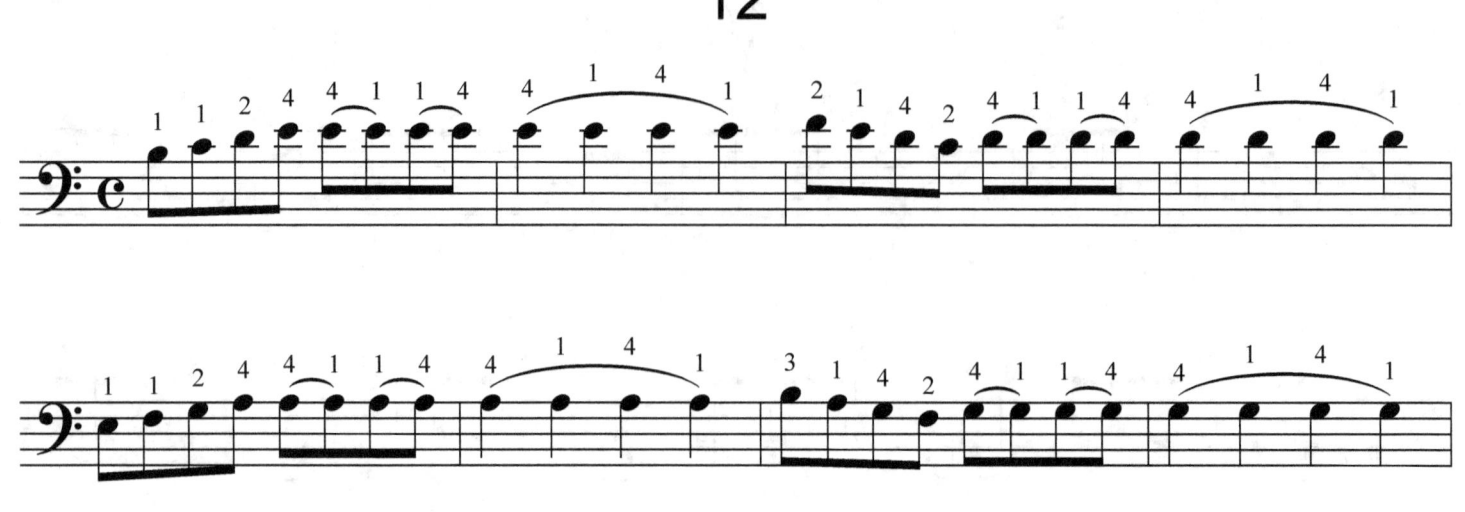

13

14

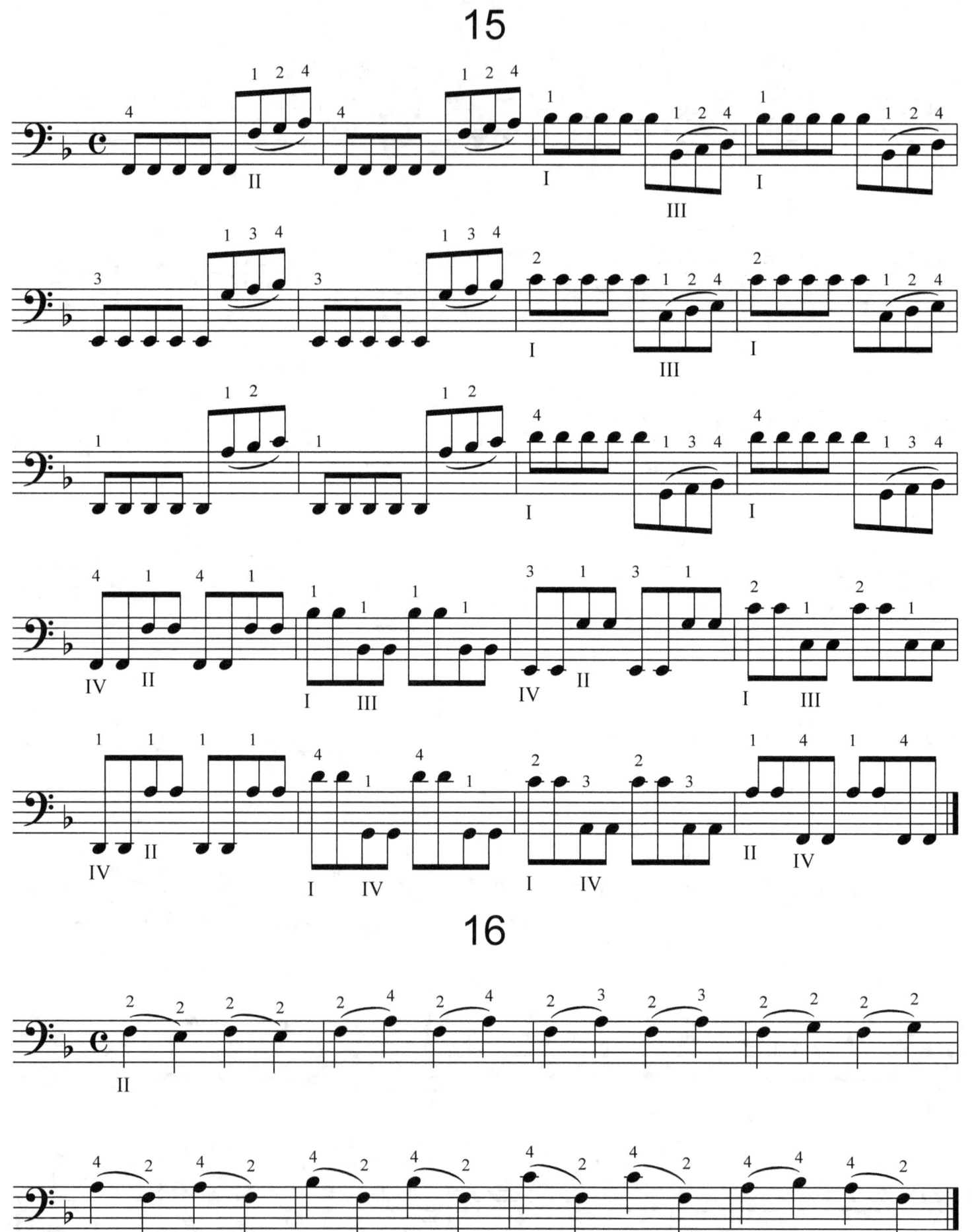

12
The Shifting Book for Cello, Part One

19

Creeping is shifting where one finger is held down on the string and another finger is moved into place below or above it. Holding 1st finger down, lift the middle two fingers and place 4th finger on the next note.

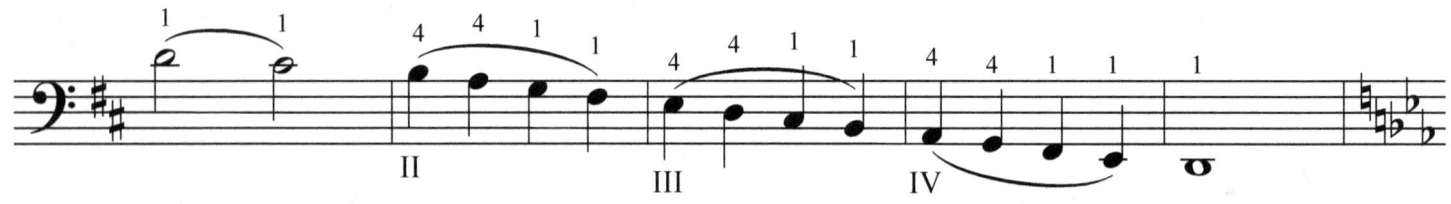

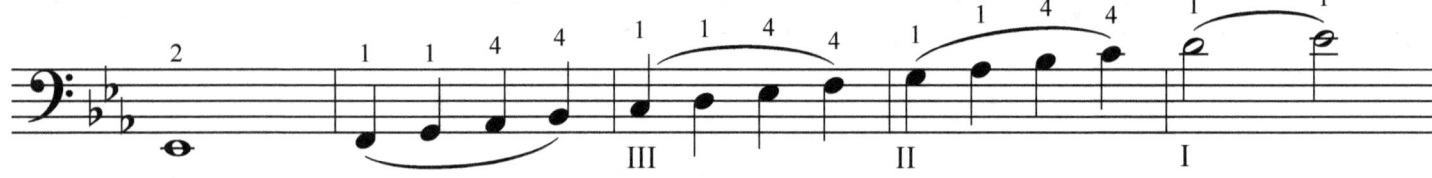

20

©2006 C. Harvey Publications All Rights Reserved.

The Shifting Book for Cello, Part One

31

The Shifting Book for Cello, Part One

First to fifth positions

42

43

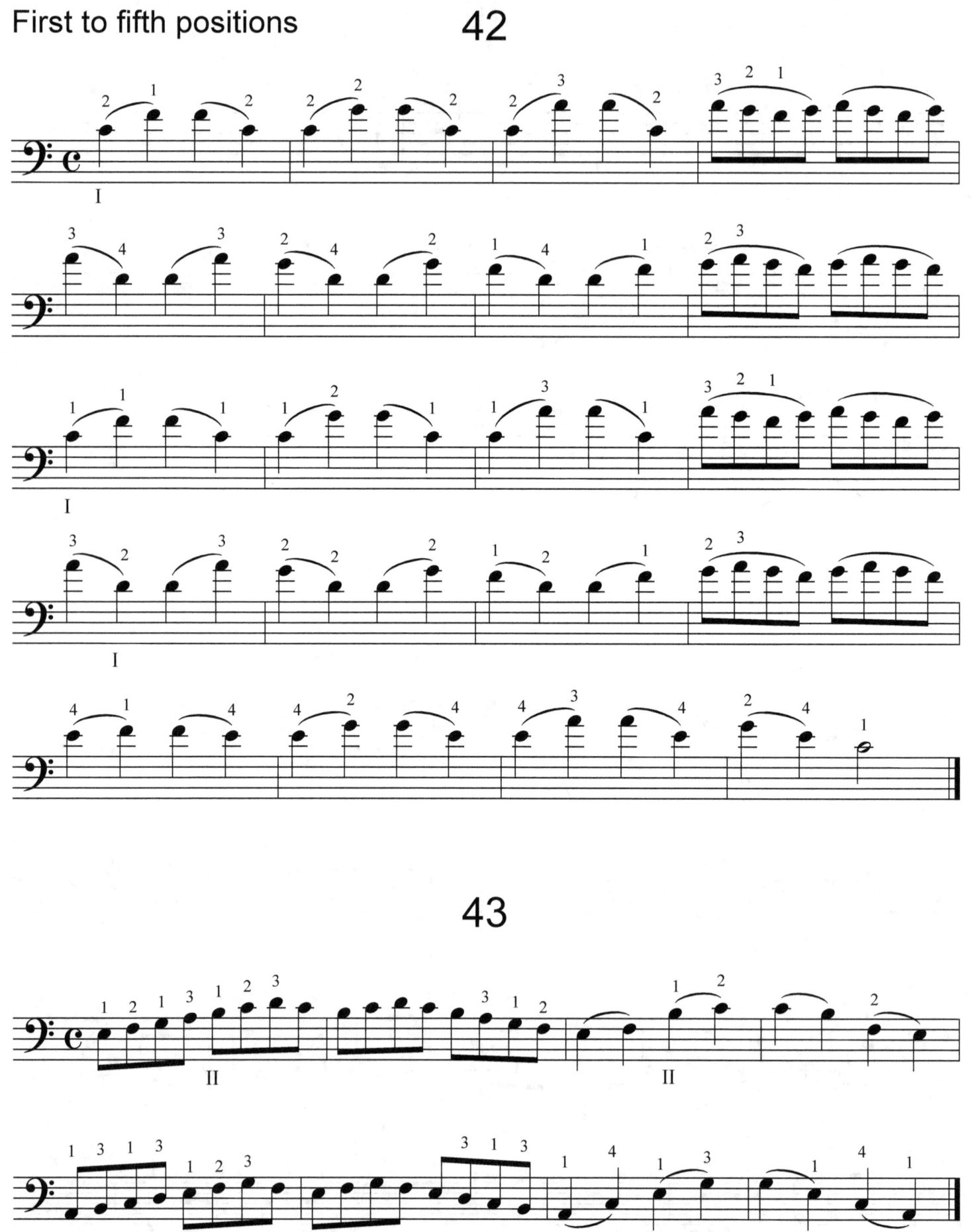

The Shifting Book for Cello, Part One

46

47

The Shifting Book for Cello, Part One

48

49

The Shifting Book for Cello, Part One

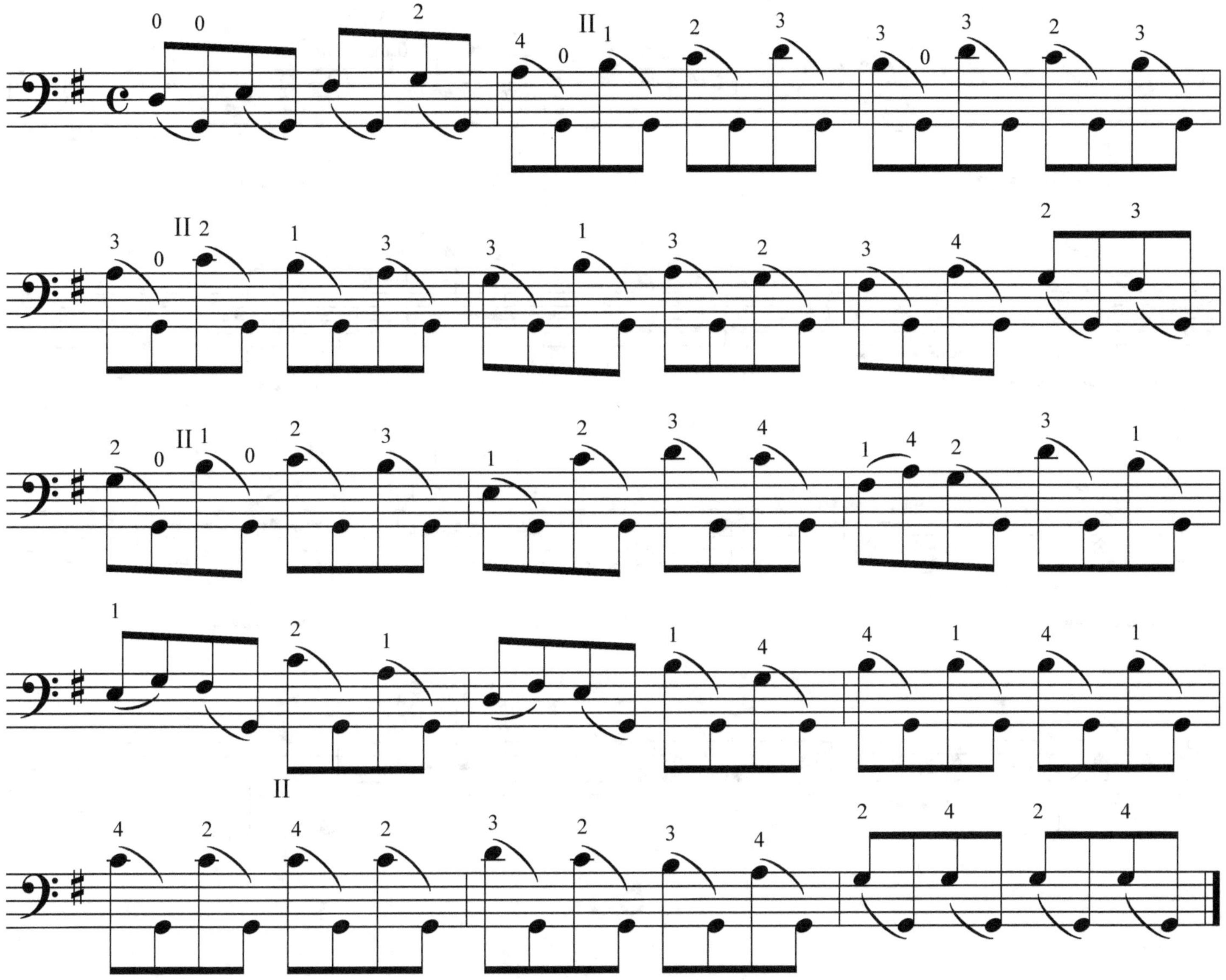

52

53

The Shifting Book for Cello, Part One

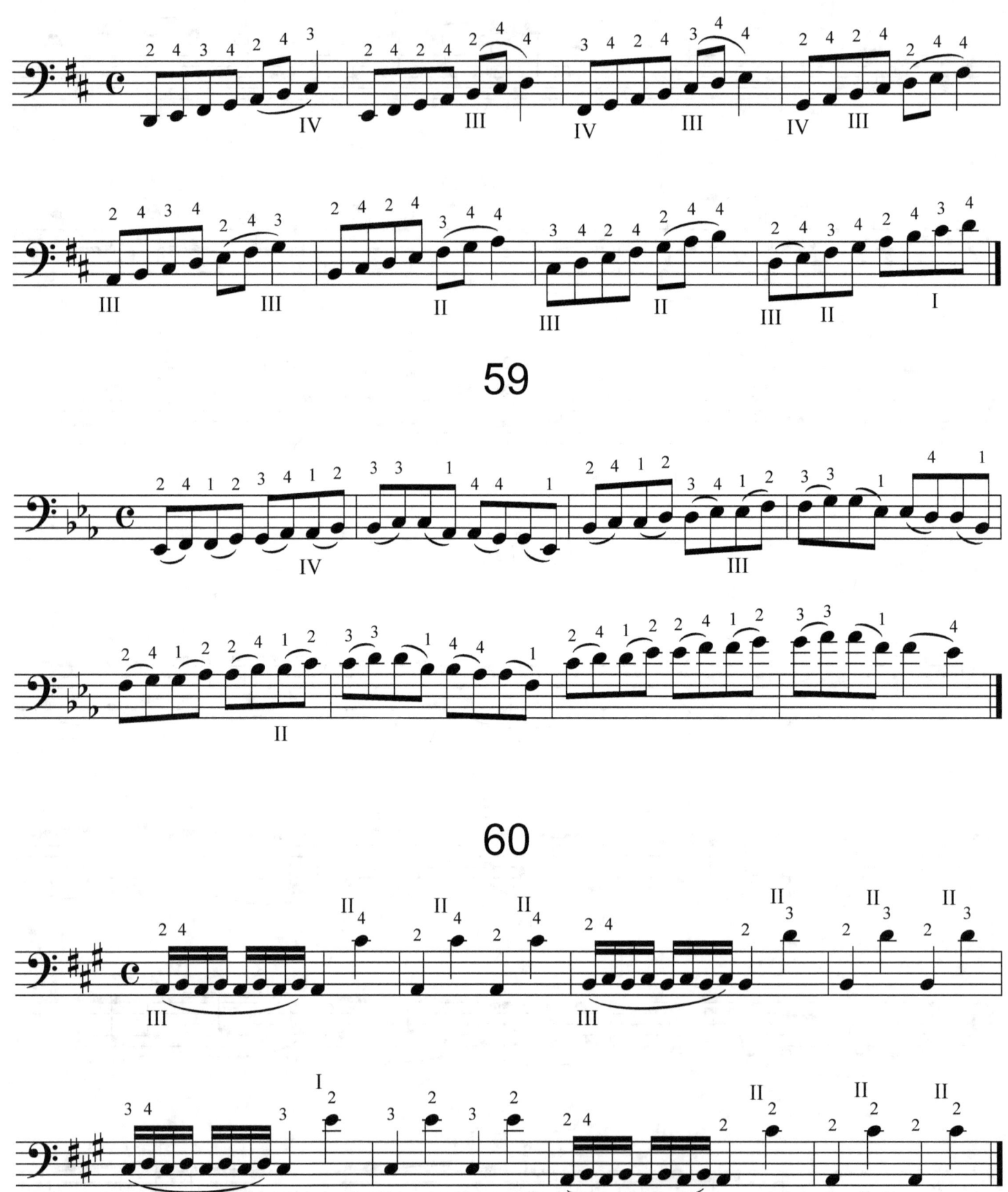

61

62

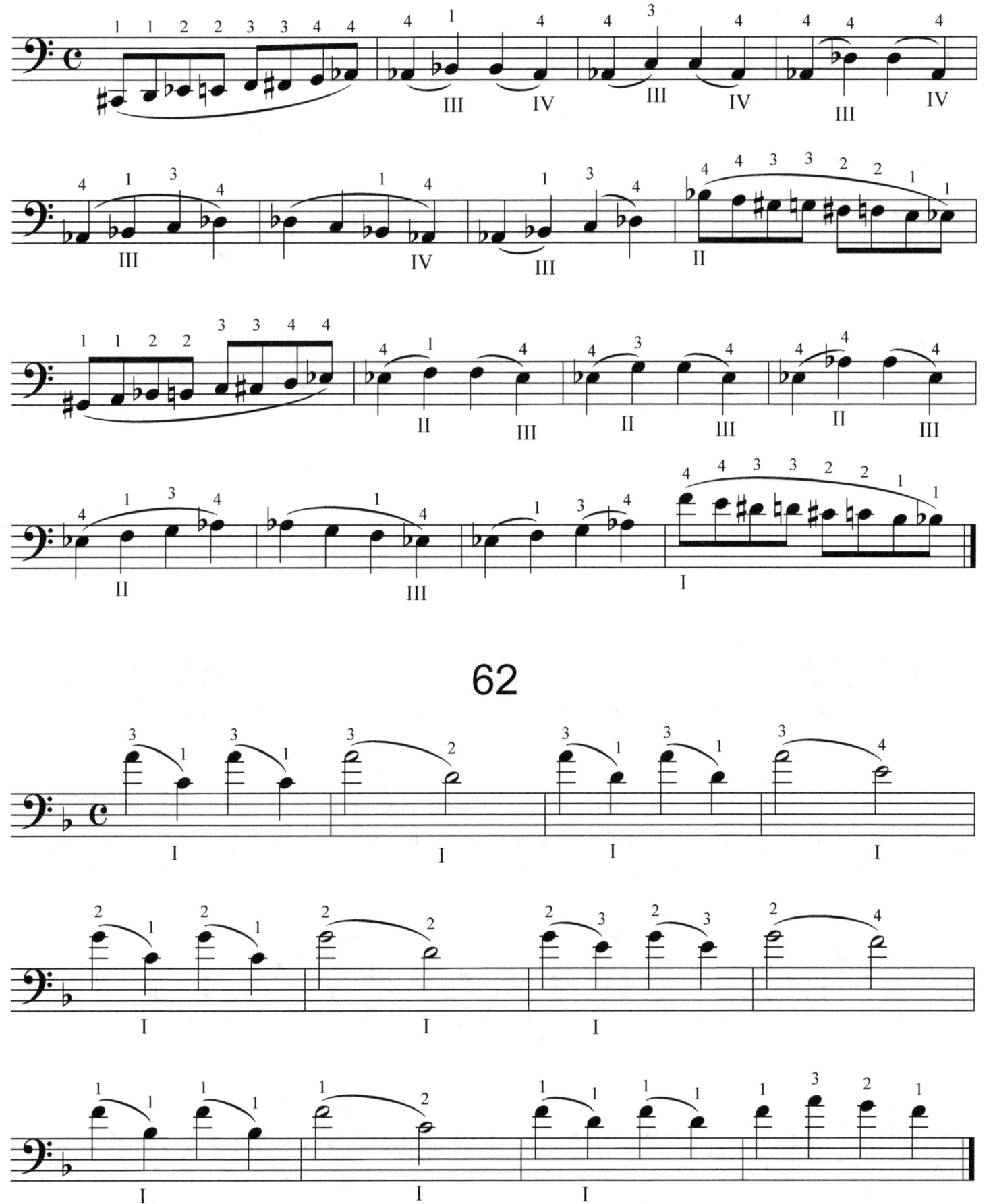

63

64

The Shifting Book for Cello, Part One

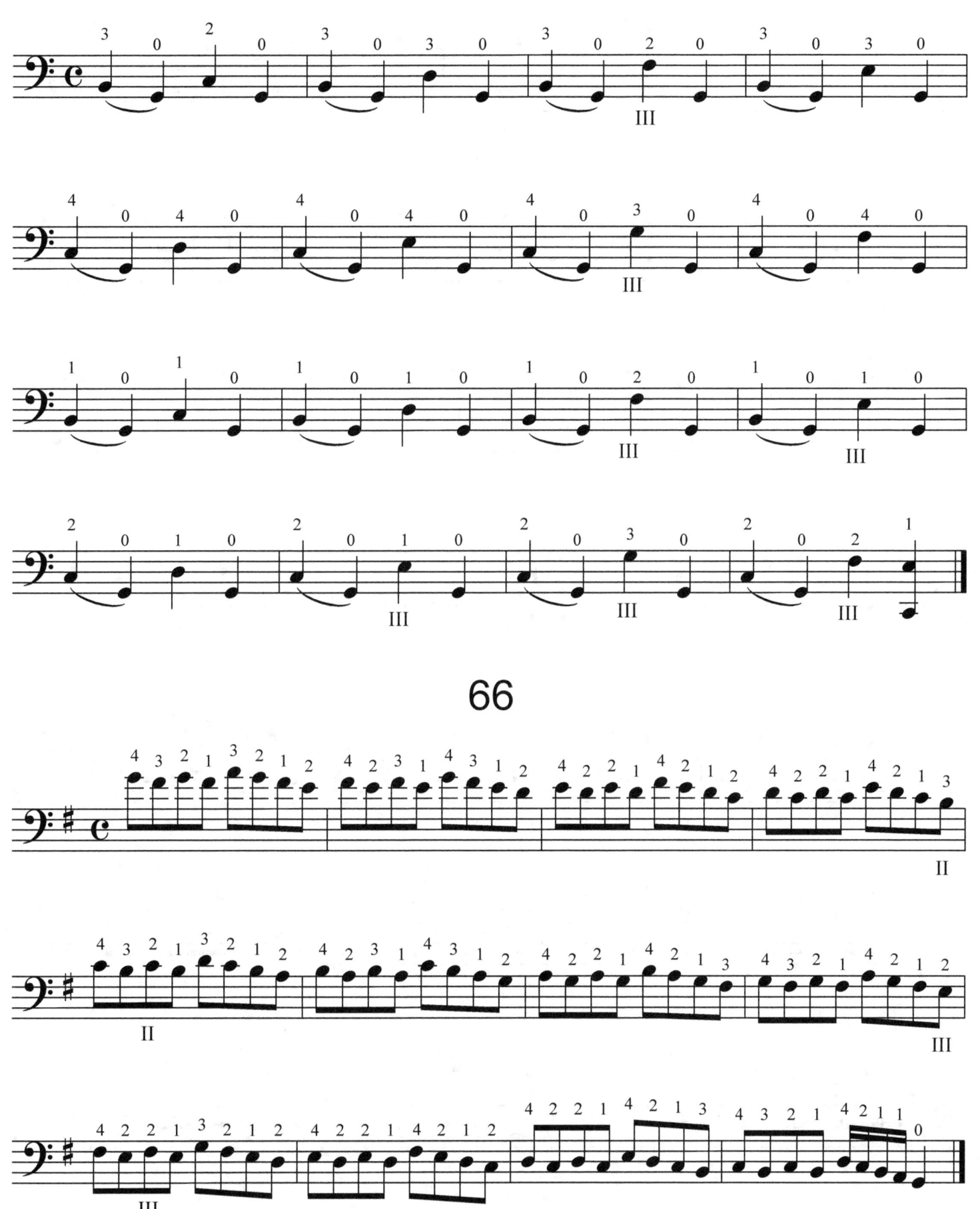

©2006 C. Harvey Publications All Rights Reserved.

67

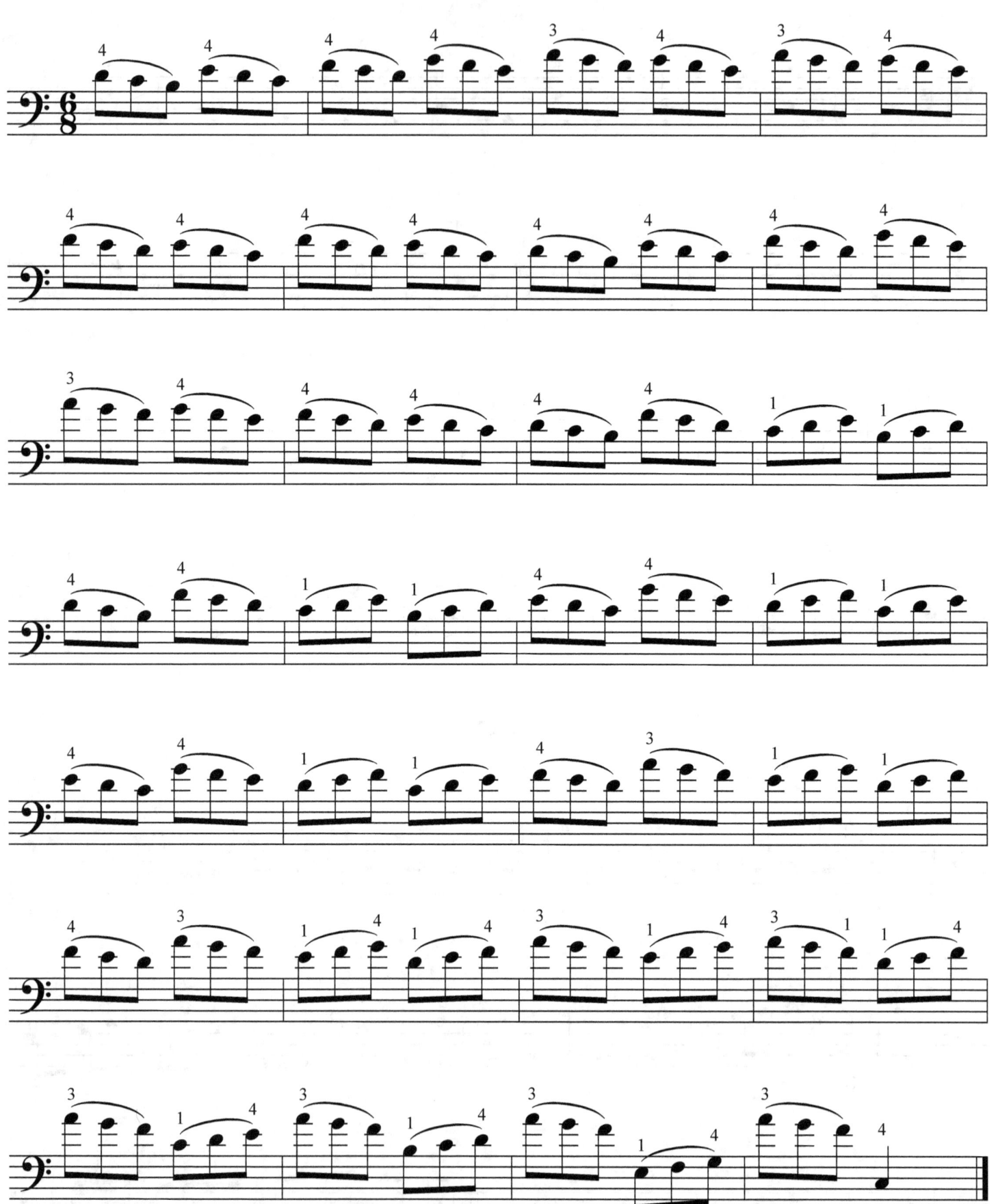

The Shifting Book for Cello, Part One

70

71

The Shifting Book for Cello, Part One

72

73

The Shifting Book for Cello, Part One

76

77

82

Also available from www.charveypublications.com: CHP348
The Romberg Sonata in C Major Study Book for Cello

Note: The Sonata is broken up into sections in this study book. The complete piece is at the back of the book.

Sonata, First Movement
Section One: Measures 1-16

Sonata Op. 43 No. 2, by Bernhard Romberg
edited by F. Jansen, C. Harvey
Exercises by Cassia Harvey

Learning the Notes/Intonation
Measures 1-3

www.ingramcontent.com/pod-product-compliance
Lightning Source LLC
Chambersburg PA
CBHW051426070526
44584CB00023B/3603